Interview

with a **SHARK**

& Other Ocean Giants Too

Written by
Andy Seed

Illustrated by
Nick East

WELBECK

Published in 2021 by Welbeck Children's Books
An imprint of Welbeck Children's Limited, part of Welbeck Publishing Group.
20 Mortimer Street London W1T 3JW

Design Manager: Emily Clarke
Designer: Sam James
Associate Publisher: Laura Knowles
Editor: Jenni Lazell

ISBN 978-1-78312-653-8

Printed in Heshan, China

10 9 8 7 6 5 4 3 2 1

Contents

Introduction

What is it like being a shark? What is a blue whale most proud of? Do giant squid attack ships? Have manta rays ever thought about wearing clothes?

You may think these are silly questions, but I ASKED THEM ANYWAY. I wanted to know the answers and if you want to know them too, then you have come to the RIGHT PLACE.

A few years ago, I accidentally invented a machine that allows me to TALK TO ANIMALS! Yes, I know it's hard to believe but, well, go on. And even better, the tranimalator (as I call it) even works UNDER WATER.

So, I took a chance, put my WET SUIT on (it's just an ordinary suit that I got wet) and jumped into the sea to INTERVIEW ten of the most amazing giant creatures found in the oceans. Then I jumped out again and put on some breathing equipment . . .

I WONDER IF HE TASTES LIKE CHICKEN . . .

Anyway, I was a bit scared. Okay, a LOT SCARED, to come face to face with a bull shark, a massive orca, and a spooky giant squid, but I chatted to them all and you can read what they had to say RIGHT HERE. I hope you enjoy it they told me some really REMARKABLE things . . .

WHAT DO YOU THINK ABOUT HUMANS?

Interview with a Bull Shark

I'm in the water right now and feeling just a teeny bit NERVOUS because my first guest is ten feet of big bite and brute force! I bring you the grumpy and magnificent BULL SHARK!

Q: What's it like being a shark?
A: Who wants to know?

Q: Uh, me. My name's Andy and I'm a writer.
A: A NUISANCE more like.

Q: So, what is it like being a shark?
A: Huh, dumb question . . . what's it like being a doofus?
It's SHARKY!

Q: Sorry, I'll try to do better.
A: Good, hurry up.

Q: Right. Why are you named after a bull?
A: Like bulls we are big, stocky, and
often moody. GRRRR!

Q: Yikes. Okay, I believe you! Uh, where do you live?
A: In water. Oh, you want more . . . If you must know I live along the coast of India in shallow seas. But bull sharks are found all over the world in places where the water is not cold.

Q: Why not in the deep sea?
A: Well, for a start, Mr. Annoying, there are plenty of fish to eat in shallow water and second, it means we are nearer to rivers.

Q: Rivers?
A: You heard me.

Q: Do you swim up them?
A: Sure. We bull sharks are special, you know. We can handle salt water in seas AND fresh water in rivers.

Q: Is there a reason you swim up rivers, or is it just for fun?
A: So many questions! Instead of talking, I might just eat you . . .

Q: But I taste horrible: a mix of sour milk and smelly socks.
A: You look horrible too.

Q: Um, anyway, why rivers?
A: Alright, whatever . . . the water in rivers is muddy—it helps us sneak up on fish without being seen. Also, our females give birth in rivers where there is less danger to the babies.

Q: What sort of danger?
A: Don't you know? Out at sea there are BIGGER sharks: tiger sharks and great whites. In rivers there's only the occasional crocodile to trouble us.

Q: Do you only eat fish?
A: Well, it's quite hard to get a burger and fries where we live . . . No, we also eat stingrays, small dolphins, and anything we can catch.

Q: Do you know any other sharks?
A: Not really—especially those losers who spend their time in the deep ocean. I've seen hammerheads and gulpers and catsharks.

Q: Haha, those names are quite funny. Do you know any more?
A: If it'll shut you up . . . There are lemon sharks, shysharks, frog sharks and pyjama sharks, plus the cookie-cutter and the spotted wobbegong.

Q: Haha, excellent! One last question: bull sharks do sometimes bite humans. Do you mean to?
A: No, although I am very tempted to give you a munch right now. We sometimes mistake humans for fish. But really, we'd rather avoid people—they catch us, kill us, and ASK US VERY ANNOYING QUESTIONS!

Q: Sorry.
A: GOOD!

Interview with a
Blue Whale

Now the BIG one! I've interviewed big names before but nothing ever as truly monstrous as this! She's as long as a basketball court and as heavy as 25 elephants. I am in awe of this guest: a mighty BLUE WHALE!

Q: How old are you?
A: Ahhhhh, aaaaaage meeeeeeans maaaaaany thiiiiiiiings . . .

Q: Uh, you speak VERY slowly. Could you maybe speed up a bit please or I'll have to row home in the dark!
A: Very well, oh tiny one.

Q: Ah, that's better! Are you very old?
A: In whale years I am 12. In human years, 90.

Q: Everyone knows you are the biggest animal on Earth. Does that matter to you?
A: We whales admire giants. But it is not size of body that matters; it is size of spirit, of heart, of understanding . . .

Q: Right . . . Uh, is it true you have no teeth?
A: It is true indeed. We do not bite, but sieve the oceans for the smallest of sea creatures.

Q: Are those the little shrimps called krill?
A: They are. They swim in pink clouds of millions, each perhaps the size of your little finger.

Q: But how can a GIGANTIC mega-beast like you survive on such, well, mini-things?
A: I have a very large mouth. I can gulp 200 tons of water then let it out, capturing thousands of krill in my mouth filter. If I eat four tons a day I can survive.

EW!

Q: Wow! you must make BIG poops!
A: Of course. It is not a good idea to swim behind me. When I let rip, I REALLY let rip! An orange plume of stink 65 feet long . . . far-flung dung . . . the jewel of stools . . . top of the plops!

Q: You seem, uh, quite proud of that.
A: Oh, um, no, no–I'm very wise and calm and gentle, remember?

Q: There are not many of you left in the world. Why's that?
A: It is true. When I was born, we were everywhere, but now we are endangered. Alas, humans are to blame.

Q: How? Why?
A: In the past, they discovered that whales can make people rich. They speared us from ships, caught us, and chopped us up for meat and to make oil. They even used our special mouth parts for fashionable dresses.

Q: How awful. I am so sorry. How did it stop?
A: There are some wise humans. Those who cared saw that we were dying out. They made the world agree to stop killing blue whales in 1967. Before then, the seas ran red . . .

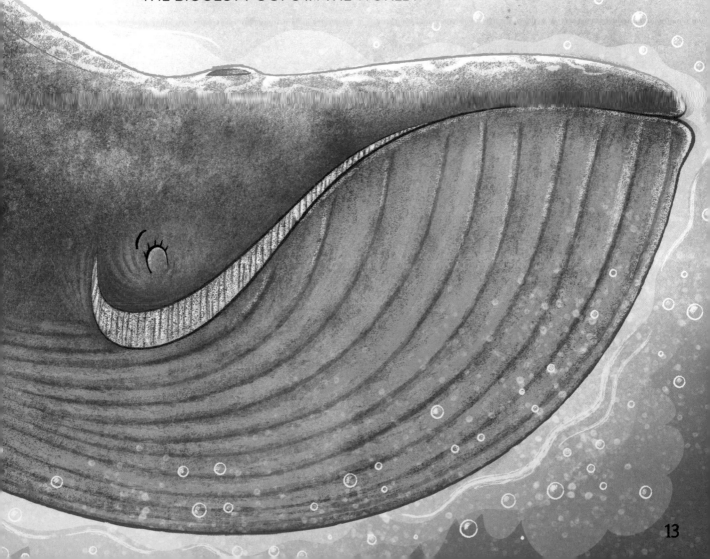

Q: And now are your numbers increasing?
A: Only very slowly. Global warming is affecting the food of the krill we depend on. The noise of ship engines brings us stress. And our bodies are riddled with tiny pieces of plastic. Once more we are in peril.

Q: This is so sad. The strange thing is that so many people love you. Did you know that?
A: Yes, we are aware. But it means more tourist boats, more noise, less peace . . .

Q: What final message do you have for the human race?
A: Just remember one thing. It is we, the blue whales, the lords of the ocean, the great salt beings of old, that make THE BIGGEST POOPS IN THE WORLD!

Interview with an Orca

Up next is a black and white sea beast you don't want to mess with. He has lots of teeth and lots of attitude. Can we give a big, warm welcome to . . . the ORCA!

Q: You are known as killer whales but is it true that you are really a type of dolphin?
A: Can I just say it's really great to be here. I'm a BIG fan! I've heard so much about you. A real pleasure, yeah!

SHOW OFF!

Q: Oh, thank you, very kind. And, uh, the question?
A: Oh, SOR-RY! I'm always doing that. My bad. Uh, what was the question?

Q: Are you a dolphin?
A: Gotcha! And the answer is . . . wait for it, wait for it . . . YES!

Q: Okay, so why are you called killer whales if you are really dolphins.
A: GOOOOOD question! So, well, the answer is . . . I dunno! No idea! It's a bit crazy, ain't it? WAIT! Maybe it's because we kinda, sorta, occasionally, uh, kill whales.

Q: But aren't whales bigger than you?
A: HEY, we're pretty big, y'know! I'm 26 feet long and weigh six tons, bro! But, yeah, some whales are bigger, some smaller but they're all GOOD TO NOSH! Those beauties taste so sweeeeet . . .

Q: What else do you eat?
A: FOOD! Now you are TALKING! Ok, we eat fish, seals, squid, weedy dolphins, turtles, sea lions, and the odd shark for a snack.

Q: You eat sharks! Aren't you scared of them?
A: Ha! Bro, you really know NOTHING! They are scared of US! We're bigger, stronger, and work together in groups—PODS!

Q: So, how do you tackle a big animal like a whale or shark?
A: So, right, we use TEAMWORK. Sometimes we tire it out, chasing it by taking turns. Sometimes we drown it by forcing it down, or we ram it to stun it. We also whack smaller things with our tails. We're smart, kid, SMART!

Q: Does anything prey on you?
A: Ha! NO WAY. We are the BOSS of the seas.

I AM NOT A TENNIS BALL!

Q: How do you keep in touch with the others in your pod?
A: Well we don't need smartphones because we use clicks, whistles and calls that work over distance. Our seeing and hearing is REALLY GOOD too.

Q: How do you feel about orcas being kept in sea life theme parks to perform shows for humans?
A: It's MEAN, man, it's BAD, it's like PRISON. We were born to be FREE! I hope it's gonna stop soon. Yeah, we're clever so we can do tricks, but we're WILD, not PETS, you know?

Q: I get the idea you're not a fan of that. Anything else you don't like?
A: WHOAH, don't get me STARTED! All the POLLUTION, like oil spills, you people spill into the sea—that makes us SICK.. And then there's the PLASTIC, and we get caught in FISHING NETS . . . Your boats are too noisy as well. SHUT UP!

Q: Oh dear, sorry Mr. Orca. I have one last question: how do you sleep?
A: RIGHT, yeah, we are very DIFFERENT from you! We rest one side of our brain at a time while the other keeps us breathing and moving slowly. Then we swap sides! GENIUS, EH? Okay, it's time to go—keep writing GOOD STUFF!

17

Interview with a
Giant Squid

Now, I must introduce you to one of the strangest and least-known creatures of the world's seas. She's not just big, she's actually a GIANT. Here, for the first time ever in interview, a GIANT SQUID!

Q: You're very mysterious—why is that?
A: It's a secret.

Q: Oh, uh, can you tell me anything?
A: Well, we are very shy and nervous you see, so we like to hide away.

Q: But you're MASSIVE! 32 feet long at least. Shouldn't you be more sure of yourself?
A: True, but, uh, we prefer to stay down in the dark depths of the ocean, out of sight.

Q: Yes, hardly anyone has ever seen a living giant squid, so why did you agree to be interviewed?
A: My mom made me do it. She said it would be good for my confidence.

Q: Okay . . . no need to worry! Are you worried?
A: Yes.

BOO!

AARRGH!

Q: Oh. Well, uh, let's talk anyway! Now then, you have eyes the size of dinner plates. Why so HUGE?
A: It's dark 1,640 feet down under the sea. Big eyes let in more light so we can find prey and spot trouble.

Q: What do you eat?
A: Fish mainly, but also smaller squid. Uh, am I doing alright?

Q: You're doing REALLY WELL. Relax! So, how do you catch fish? I can't see a mouth. In fact, I'm wondering how you're talking right now . . .
A: Ah, well, to catch fish we grab them with our two special feeding tentacles. Mine are 26 feet long and have suckers on the end with sharp teeth to grip. Then we pull the fish into our beak.

Q: You have a beak! Are you a bird??
A: Oh no, a mollusk. Snails and slugs are mollusks, too.
But we are more closely related to the octopus.

Q: Do you have eight arms then?
A: Yes, eight strong arms and two longer tentacles as well.

Q: Are the arms for swimming?
A: Oh, no, no, no–we use them to fight off other squid and defend
against attack. We move around by squirting water out of a funnel.

**Q: Nice! You mentioned attack: who are
your predators? They must be REALLY
big to tackle you!**
A: Oh dear, I was afraid you'd ask
about that . . .

Q: It's OK, you're safe here. Well, there are a few sharks and killer whales around but they're very friendly really.
A: Oh no, oooh, I'm all shaky now . . . And I don't like to speak about the things that eat us. Sperm whales. There, I've said it now. They're enormous, strong, and fast and have lots of teeth. We don't stand a chance against them . . .

Q: Poor you. No sperm whales here today, though (thank goodness). Uh, to change the subject, what are your three top giant squid facts you can tell us?
A: Erm, ooh, alright . . . One, we can squirt ink to confuse our enemies. Two, we have teeth on our tongues. Three, we have three hearts.

Q: Amazing! Finally, story writers in the past have described MONSTER giant squid that attack ships and sink them. Do you do that?
A: Yes.

Q: Really??
A: No we don't—a sloth told me to say yes. Silly goose. Erm, please can I go now? I gotta pee.

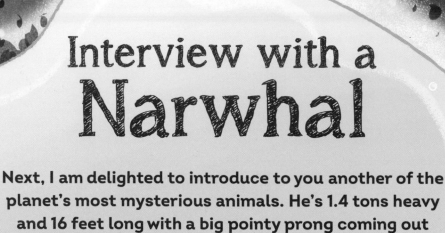

Interview with a Narwhal

Next, I am delighted to introduce to you another of the planet's most mysterious animals. He's 1.4 tons heavy and 16 feet long with a big pointy prong coming out of his lip, yes, it's the legendary NARWHAL!

Q: Did you know that people call you "the unicorn of the sea?"
A: We know that humans have always chased us for our tusks, of course, but unicorn–is that a kind of horse?

Q: Correct! I think it's because your tusks were thought to have magical powers in days of old. I like the way your answer kind of rhymed.
A: Hehe, you know, we don't mean to rhyme–it just seems to happen some of the time.

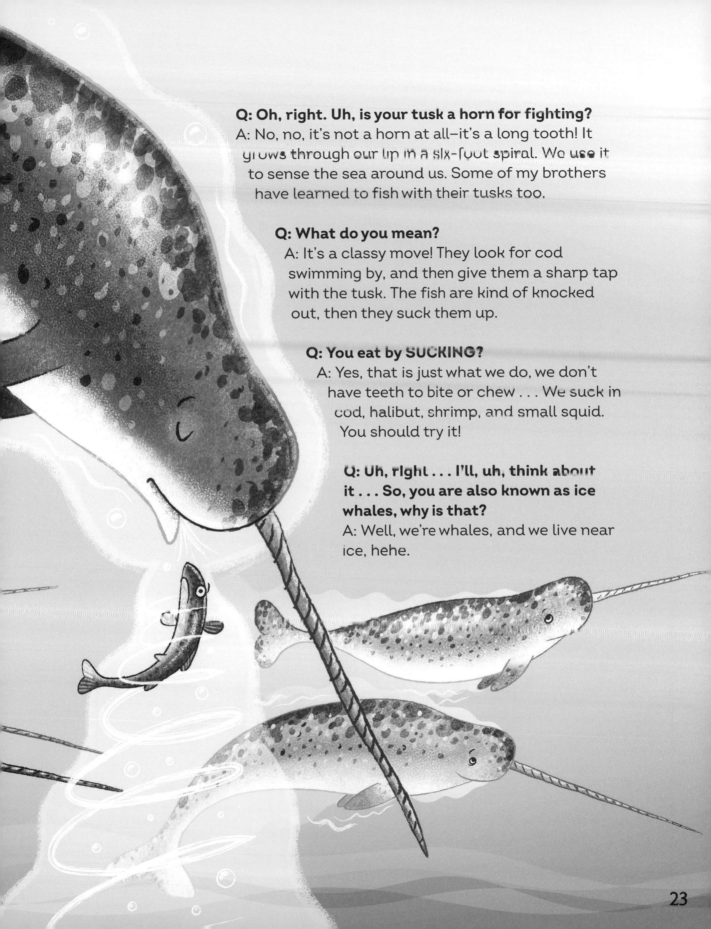

Q: Oh, right. Uh, is your tusk a horn for fighting?
A: No, no, it's not a horn at all—it's a long tooth! It grows through our lip in a six-foot spiral. We use it to sense the sea around us. Some of my brothers have learned to fish with their tusks too.

Q: What do you mean?
A: It's a classy move! They look for cod swimming by, and then give them a sharp tap with the tusk. The fish are kind of knocked out, then they suck them up.

Q: You eat by SUCKING?
A: Yes, that is just what we do, we don't have teeth to bite or chew . . . We suck in cod, halibut, shrimp, and small squid. You should try it!

Q: Uh, right . . . I'll, uh, think about it . . . So, you are also known as ice whales, why is that?
A: Well, we're whales, and we live near ice, hehe.

Q: Can you tell me a bit more?
A: Okay. We live in the cold Arctic seas around Canada, Russia, and Norway. There in winter, the sea freezes over—it can be very dangerous for narwhals like me.

Q: How is it dangerous?
A: Well, we find fish to eat around the ice, but if we spend too long there, the sea can freeze above us and then we can't surface to breathe.

Q: How frightening to be trapped! Has it ever happened to you?
A: Just once and it was NOT nice. We had to swim almost a mile to find a hole in the ice.

Q: I've interviewed a few animals that eat whales (sorry). Which ones do you have to watch out for?
A: You're right—some of them are NASTY. Killer whales trap us in bays sometimes. Polar bears grab our babies through ice holes, and giant Greenland sharks catch us sometimes too, those meanies.

Q: What else can you tell me about yourself?
A: We can dive very deep—over 5,000 feet. We don't like people or noise or ships, and we change our color from dark to white as we get older.

Q: Do you have any hobbies?
A: Yes: stamp collecting, yoga, and flower arranging.

Q: REALLY?
A: No, not really.

Q: Finally, what's your favorite country? Iceland maybe?
A: Of course not. It's Wales!

Interview with a
Manta Ray

Wow, my next ocean giant is almost 20 feet wide! She's like nothing else you've ever seen: flat, flexible, and flowing, it's the wonderful MANTA RAY!

Q: How are you?
A: I'm lush! And SO excited to be in your book. You will send me a signed copy, won't you? A waterproof one.

Q: Uh, I will see what I can do . . . Right, I was very surprised to read that you're sometimes called the devilfish—you're not nasty and evil are you?
A: Me? No! I'm kind and gentle and sweet. Would you like a cup of tea and some cake?

Q: You can make tea??
A: No, I was just being polite. I thought that's what humans like.

Q: Well, true, but where does the devilfish name come from?
A: Oh, sorry, yes. That's pure nonsense—it's because we have two fins on our head that look like horns when we roll them up, that's all. By the way, I like your shirt.

Q: Oh, thank you. Manta rays don't wear clothes—have you ever thought about it?
A: I would really like a top hat but there are no stores in the tropical seas where we live, sadly.

Q: Right. I notice that you don't swim by moving your tail, like most fish. How do you do it?
A: Very good question. We use our large pectoral fins a bit like birds' wings. We move them so that they push water back. It's more elegant, don't you think?

Q: Oh yes, I agree. Uh, did you know there's a small fish stuck to your belly?
A: Indeed. A remora. A sucker fish. I'm a peaceful being but those things do make me SPIT. They just want a free ride! Unwelcome hitchhikers. Stowaways.
Rascals! Smelly noodles!

Q: Are there any fish you do like?
A: Oh yes. Terribly sorry for my dreadful language, by the way —I must apologize. Right, fish. I like the ones I eat and I like the ones that clean me.

Q: Clean you?
A: Just so. We stop by reefs where certain small fish pick parasites and dead skin off our bodies. It's a most delightful free service.

Q: What else do you eat?
A: I can't stand curry. We go for small things: tiny plankton near the surface and small fish deeper down, below 650 feet.

Q: How do manta rays feel about human beings?
A: Well you are very nice but some are the worst.

Q: Why?
A: It's the tourist divers who try and grab us by the tail or fins to be towed along. It takes the mucus off our skin.

Q: Wow, you're covered in SNOT?
A: Many fish are—it's why we're so slippery! It helps protect us from bacteria and things.

Q: Ah, I see. Why else are people a problem for you?
A: They use giant fishing nets and sometimes we get tangled in them. Then there is all the trash they dump in the oceans . . .

Q: Yes, it's very bad, sorry. We are trying to do something about it.
A: We are really glad to hear it, thanks, dearest.

Q: Is there anything else you'd like to tell our young readers?
A: Yes. Don't PEE IN THE SEA—I have to drink that stuff!

Interview with an
Ocean Sunfish

This underwater guest is one of the most curious creatures you may ever see. She's a real whopper in the ocean world and can now talk to us for the first time ever: yes, it's the OCEAN SUNFISH!

Q: Do you know why you are called a sunfish?
A: No.

Q: Oh, well, my research says it could be because you are sun-shaped. Other people think it's because you float on the surface of the water sometimes, like you are sunbathing. Which is it?
A: Dunno.

Q: OK, well, um, can you tell me something about yourself?
A: Sure.

Q: Like what?
A: I don't like sea lions.

Q: Why's that?
A: They sometimes bite me. And sharks and orcas do it too.

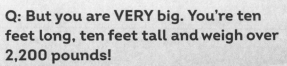

Q: But you are VERY big. You're ten feet long, ten feet tall and weigh over 2,200 pounds!

A: Yes, but I am slow and I have no teeth to bite back.

Q: **How do you manage with no tail?**

A: How do YOU manage with no tail?

Q: **Good point. Uh, you have many nicknames, I found out. Your scientific name is *mola mola* which means millstone; some people call you moonfish and in German you're known as the "swimming head." Did you know that?**

A: I do now, but I don't care.

Q: What do you care about?
A: Finding food, finding a mate, finding ways to get rid of parasites in my skin. Oh, and avoiding plastic bags.

Q: Are plastic bags a problem?
A: Yes, in the sea they look like jellyfish and I sometimes eat them. They make me very ill. I say STOP USING THEM!

Q: I agree. Um, you mentioned parasites in your skin. What are they?
A: Small creatures that live in me and on me, like worms and lice. They itch, they make me unwell, and I WANT THEM GONE! There are some kind fish and birds that remove them for me.

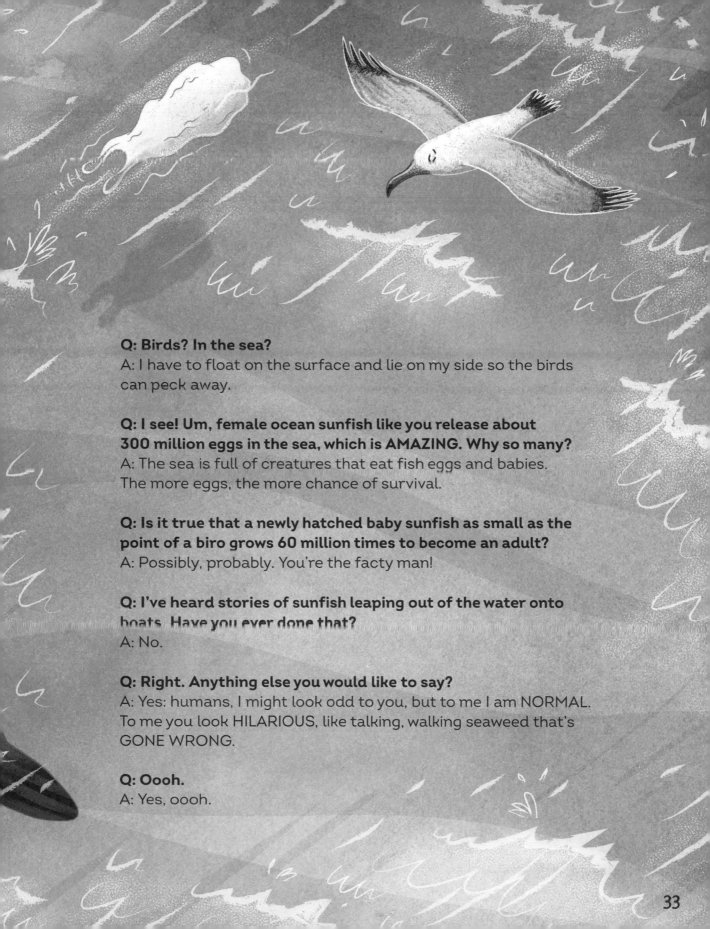

Q: Birds? In the sea?
A: I have to float on the surface and lie on my side so the birds can peck away.

Q: I see! Um, female ocean sunfish like you release about 300 million eggs in the sea, which is AMAZING. Why so many?
A: The sea is full of creatures that eat fish eggs and babies. The more eggs, the more chance of survival.

Q: Is it true that a newly hatched baby sunfish as small as the point of a biro grows 60 million times to become an adult?
A: Possibly, probably. You're the facty man!

Q: I've heard stories of sunfish leaping out of the water onto boats. Have you ever done that?
A: No.

Q: Right. Anything else you would like to say?
A: Yes: humans, I might look odd to you, but to me I am NORMAL. To me you look HILARIOUS, like talking, walking seaweed that's GONE WRONG.

Q: Oooh.
A: Yes, oooh.

Interview with an
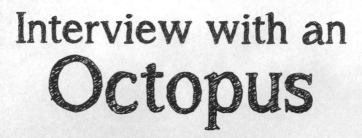
Octopus

The guest I am going to interview now is unmistakable. Squishy, amazing, smart, mysterious and able to do hold eight ice creams at once, it's the remarkable OCTOPUS!

Q: What kind of octopus are you?
A: A really good one! I'm actually a Giant Pacific octopus, but friends call me Soldier because I'm well-armed!

Q: Oh . . . because you have eight arms . . .
I get it. But aren't they legs? Or tentacles?
A: Well, they do everything, so they're sort of all three. I can even taste with them!

Q: Wow. I know you have no bones, but is it true that octopuses have blue blood?
A: Yes! I've got thousands of suckers too, so when grumpy fish say, "You suck," it's true!

Q: You seem to like jokes. Can you tell us one of your best ones?
A: Okay, okay, okay . . . Why did the octopus blush?

Q: I don't know. Why?
A: It saw the bottom of the sea! Haha!

Q: It made me laugh. Uh, you can actually change color, can't you?
A: Sure can. We change our skin to blend right in! Camouflage helps us sneak up on prey and hide from hungry dolphins and sea otters.

Q: What do you eat?
A: Prawns, crabs, lobsters, fish, bristle worms, clams, and crispy noodles.

Q: Really??
A: No, I lied about the noodles, haha.

HERE'S WHAT I THINK OF YOUR JOKES!

Q: I read in a book that octopuses don't live very long. Is that true?
A: Uh-oh . . . Yes, it's right. Females die soon after laying eggs and males die after mating although the female sometimes eats the male before she croaks. Not a very romantic last date, eh?

Q: Woah, I'm glad I'm not an octopus!
A: Yeah, but we can do cool things like shoot ink at attackers. And if we lose an arm to a hungry fish, we just grow a new one—we don't need a doctopus!

Q: Time for another joke?
A: Yeah, yeah, yeah! Right, how do you make an octopus laugh?

Q: Go on, how?
A: You give it ten tickles.

Q: Ten Tickles? Oh, tentacles! Shocker! Can you tell me more facts about yourself?
A: Of course! We have a mouth with a sharp beak, we are venomous, we have large brains, and we very rarely travel by taxi.

Q: Do you only walk, or can you swim?
A: We can do both. To swim we squirt water through our siphon—it's like jet propulsion, but without the noise and fumes!

Q: Where do you live?
A: Well, I can't afford a house or an apartment so I live in a cozy underwater den which I made myself.

Q: Sound wonderful! Do you have one last joke for us?
A: Yessss! What's an octopus's favorite book?

Q: I don't know. What is it?
A: DIARY OF A WIMPY SQUID!

Q: I am speechless.
A: Goodbye dear fans, it's been fun, take care, sweet dreams—I LOVE YOU ALL!

Interview with a Conger Eel

Now it's time to meet a fearsome hunter that lurks in the depths of the seas around Europe. Six feet long, with a bite like a bulldog, it's the CONGER EEL!

Q: You look a bit like a snake. Are you a snake?
A: What's a snake?

Q: It looks like you but usually lives on land. They have scales but no fins. What do you think?
A: I have fins but no scales and I live in the sea. And I'm an eel. Does that answer the question?

Q: Yes, thanks. Why do you like living in holes among rocks and in shipwrecks?
A: They are good places to hide so we can ambush fish and shrimps or cuttlefish to eat. We like to stay in the dark, out of sight, then it's BLAM! Then CHOMP, CHOMP, CHOMP. Do you ambush your food?

Q: Um, well, I can't say I have ever hidden behind a display of canned tomatoes in the supermarket and jumped out on a frozen pizza, no. Do you eat anything else?
A: Dead stuff on the seabed. We're not fussy.

Q: What is your dream?
A: You mean, do I have nightmares about running down main street naked? No, I don't wear pants anyway.

Q: Sorry, I mean do you have an ambition?
A: Yeah. To SMASH into a MASSIVE herring and GOBBLE it all up.

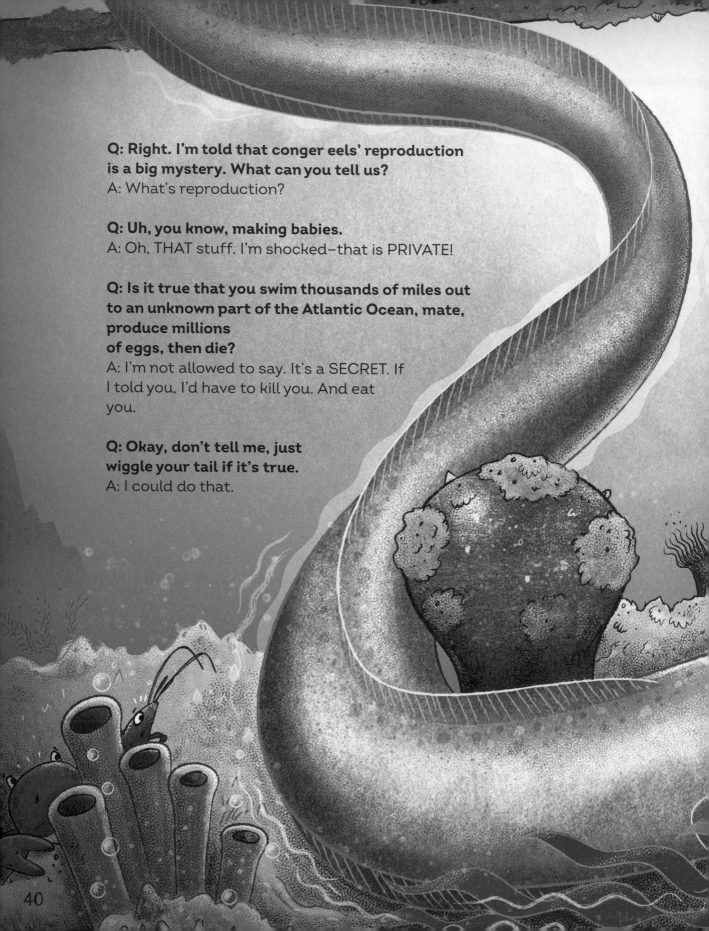

Q: Right. I'm told that conger eels' reproduction is a big mystery. What can you tell us?
A: What's reproduction?

Q: Uh, you know, making babies.
A: Oh, THAT stuff. I'm shocked—that is PRIVATE!

Q: Is it true that you swim thousands of miles out to an unknown part of the Atlantic Ocean, mate, produce millions of eggs, then die?
A: I'm not allowed to say. It's a SECRET. If I told you, I'd have to kill you. And eat you.

Q: Okay, don't tell me, just wiggle your tail if it's true.
A: I could do that.

Q: Thank you for that wiggle! Now, back to food: what is your favorite ice cream flavor?
A: Uhh, can you get squid and crab?

Q: Probably not. I've noticed you have sharp teeth but also an ability to sort of suck in food like an underwater turbo vacuum cleaner. How do you do that?
A: I'm not sure. I was just born able to do it.

Q: Hmmm. You are a fish, but it looks like you swim differently than other fish. Is that right?
A: Ah, this I KNOW! Most fish kind of wiggle their body from side to side, especially the tail, to push water behind them, but we eels are very long so instead we create a wave which moves down our body. If we reverse the wave we can swim backward—other fish can't do that.

Q: Interesting! OK, final question, and it's a good one. Do congers ever do the conga?
A: I have no idea what you're talking about.

Q: Fair enough.
A: I'm off.

Interview with an Anglerfish

My final interview is with one of the strangest and creepiest animals I have ever met. It's around three and a half feet long but with one of the biggest, nastiest mouths on the planet, the ANGLERFISH!

Q: You look angry. Are you angry?
A: YES! Because it's so stinkingly hard to find food where I live!

Q: You mean in the sea?
A: Not just 'in the sea'! I mean WAY DOWN in the deep, over 6,500 feet, where it's DARK and COLD.

Q: Oh, I see. So, how do you find something to eat down there?
A: Gah, I have to CATCH IT—that's why I'm an angler fish. I thought you'd know that . . .

Q: Do you have a fishing rod?
A: Yes! Well, it's a special spine fixed to my body—a lure.

Q: Ah, that kind of dangly thing above your head?
A: Yes, THAT. Some anglerfish can wiggle it, so it looks like a small animal, good to eat.

Q: But how do other creatures see it in the dark?
A: It lights up. The end has glowing bacteria in it. I just wish it WORKED BETTER!

Q: Smart! So, what kind of animals does the light attract?
A: Fish, squid, shrimps, sea worms, that kind of stuff. I can open my big mouth REALLY wide and then BAM! Snatch 'em in! This talk is making me HUNGRY!

Q: Why do you have such big teeth, grandma?
A: What??

Q: Sorry, it just reminded me of *Little Red Riding Hood*.
A: Buffoon! I need these sharp teeth to grasp slippery fish.
And if I eat something bigger than me it's going to try
and ESCAPE! The teeth keep it PRISONER.

**Q: Excuse me, did you just say you can eat something
bigger than yourself?**
A: Yeah! Grrrr, do I have to explain EVERYTHING?

Q: Uh, well, that's kind of the idea of an interview . . .
A: Oh, sorry. Well, my mouth opens extra-wide and my belly
is stretchy and my bones are soft and bendy so I can gobble
BIG things.

**Q: Smart move. So, you don't chase food—
you wait until it comes to you. A bit like
a supermarket delivery?**
A: A what? You humans are WEIRD . . .
Anyway, yeah, I'm a fish that fishes,
not a hunter that hunts. And if there's
little food around we have to save
energy by drifting in the ocean.

Q: Are you male or female?
A: I'm a female—that's why I'm big.
The males are tiny little things.

**Q: Do they bite you? I heard about
that somewhere.**
A: It's true. With some types of
anglerfish, the little guys bury their
teeth into the girl and then stay fixed
on permanently.

Q: Eeurrgh, how do they eat?
A: Their bodies kind of fuse with the females', so they share blood and food. The males lose their eyes and other organs, though. Gross, huh?

Q: Gross indeed.
A: I'd better go now. I'm HUNGRY!

HE'S NICE, BUT A BIT CLINGY

How you can help

Animals are amazing, aren't they? There are so many different types and they have such interesting lives. I hope you enjoyed meeting some of the sea creatures in this book as much as I did.

Sadly, some of the ocean giants interviewed here might not be around in the future. Yes, they are ENDANGERED. That means that numbers of them are lower than they should be.

So, what can we all do to help save these wonderful animals? Well, if we LOOK AFTER OUR PLANET better, that will be a start. Here are some ways that you can make sure that blue whales, manta rays, and more are still around for years to come.

1. Get active
It helps to understand what the ocean is like.
So, ask to have a trip to the seaside:

- ≈ Walk along the shore—go bird spotting
- ≈ Visit a sea life center
- ≈ Look in rock pools
- ≈ Explore a beach—find evidence of wildlife

2. Join a local group
There are awesome groups of people everywhere who work to care for the environment. You can often become a junior member of organizations that protect animals, such as wildlife trusts.

3. Clean a beach
If you live near the coast then you might be able to join with other people to help keep a local beach clean. It's important that you ask a parent or guardian to go with you.
- ≈ Find out if there is a local voluntary group that does beach cleaning
- ≈ Take a bag each and do a family bottle search: use gloves or litter pickers to collect plastic bottles or other plastic waste. Take them for recycling.
- ≈ Remember, do not put any trash or plastic collected in litter bins— these can get too full and overflow back onto the shore!

4. Raise money

Nature charities and big organizations like WWF (World Wildlife Fund)
depend on money to do important conservation work, protecting the
wildlife that is under threat. Here's how you can help them:

    ≈ Adopt an endangered animal with WWF or a similar group
    ≈ Ask a teacher if your school can help with raising money for wildlife
    ≈ Find out about smaller charities which help animals, such as
    seabirds and seals

5. Help prevent pollution

Making and using most things involves energy and can create nasty pollution.
Transport adds to climate change too, and all of this affects wild animals.
Here are some ways to REDUCE pollution:

    ≈ Turn off lights when you're not using them
    ≈ Unplug chargers
    ≈ Switch off devices when you've finished with them
    ≈ Walk or bike short journeys, instead of going by car
    ≈ Reuse and recycle as much as possible
    ≈ Don't drop litter

6. Avoid using plastic

We now know that tiny pieces of plastic are getting into seas all over Earth.
Many sea creatures end up swallowing them, which does them no good at all.

    ≈ Instead of plastic bags, use any bag that can be used lots of times
    ≈ For drinks, use a bottle which can be refilled
    ≈ Use bars of soap instead of shampoo and gel in plastic bottles

7. Tell our leaders

It's up to the people in charge to make changes that help wildlife. You can
encourage them by writing letters which show that you care about protecting
sea life and the oceans. Ask a parent or guardian how to do this.

8. Learn more

This book has helped you understand a little about the lives of some
special animals. Use your local library (where the books are free to borrow)
to find out more, and to discover what else you can do to protect
OUR AMAZING PLANET.

47

Quiz

Can you answer these fun questions about each of the ten sea creatures in the book? Give it a try! All the information is on the pages somewhere. Answers are at the bottom of the page.

1. Bull sharks can be found in which surprising places?
a) Rock pools   b) Shoe stores   c) Rivers   d) Your bath

2. What color is blue whale poop?
a) Blue   b) Orange   c) Green   d) Yellow with purple spots

3. What is a group of orcas called?
a) A pod   b) A pid   c) A ped   d) A pud

4. How many tentacles does a giant squid have?
a) 2   b) 8   c) 10   d) 731

5. What is a narwhal tusk?
a) A giant tooth   b) A horn   c) A special bone   d) A TV antenna

6. What are manta rays covered in?
a) Scales   b) Pimples   c) Limpets   d) Mucus

7. What do people in Germany call the ocean sunfish?
a) "Swimming head"   b) "Swimming bottom"
c) "Egg face"   d) "Floating pie"

8. Which of these is a favorite food of the octopus?
a) Carrot   b) Crab   c) Otter   d) Trifle

9. What can the conger eel do that most fish can't?
a) Read and write   b) Change color   c) Tie shoelaces   d) Swim backward

10. What makes an anglerfish's lure glow in the dark?
a) Bacteria   b) Batteries   c) Coal   d) Luminous blood

Answers: 1c 2b 3a 4a 5a 6d 7a 8b 9d 10a